THE
LIFE GUIDE SERIES

Selected Works of
CLYDE M. NARRAMORE, Ed.D.

Volume Five

SECTION I: How to Study and be Successful in School

SECTION II: Improving Your Self-Confidence

GOOD WILL PUBLISHERS, Inc.
Gastonia, North Carolina

How to Study and be Successful in School
Copyright 1961 by Clyde M. Narramore

Improving Your Self-Confidence
Copyright 1961 by Clyde M. Narramore

Printed in the United States of America

Index

SECTION I: How to Study and be Successful in School

Success in School 5
You Can Study Less 7
Where to Study 9
A Schedule Saves Time 11
Briefing for Study 13
The Mastery of SQ3R 14
Increasing Your Reading Skill 18
Taking and Keeping Notes 21
Learning to Memorize 25
Using the Library 28
Writing Themes and Reports 32
When You Give That Speech 34
Preparing for and Taking Examinations 39
Impressing Your Teacher 43
What About Your SQ? 46

SECTION II: Improving Your Self-Confidence

Competence and Confidence 53
Feeling at Ease 55
Conversational Skills 58
Confidence Through Christ 63
Understanding Your Feelings 72
Seeking Professional Help 75
In Retrospect 76

THE LIFE GUIDE SERIES: Volume 5

SECTION I:

How to Study and be Successful in School

1 | Success in School

If you are studying in school, taking evening or summer courses, or in fact, acquiring any sort of formal education, you need the information in this book. In all probability, you already know much about studying, but, like most people, you want to know more.

There are good ways and poor ways to do anything — even studying. Are there ways in which you might improve? If so, this book may prove a gold mine to you. The suggestions given here can affect all the study you will ever do.

Is this book for poor students? No, not necessarily. It's for everyone — for you, if you want to *learn* how to study; for you, if you would like to *improve*.

Learning Is Fun

God has given every human being a desire to learn and to gain knowledge. Call it curiosity, inquisitiveness, or whatever you may, there is real joy in learning. Man craves it.

Studying need not be boresome. In fact it can be a lot of fun. It is mental stimulation that keeps a person growing intellectually. Knowing *how* to study increases your enjoyment. When you can take a book, read it quickly, and know how to select the main points, you enjoy doing it. This brings a real sense of satisfaction.

Studying Pays Off

One thing is sure: it pays to study.

Those who make the best grades in school usually make the best incomes after they leave the campus. Just look around, and you will see that most of those who go to the top are the same ones who did well in school. Surveys show that the earning capacity of employees is closely related to their school grades.

Why is this? First, employers are impressed by marks and they offer better jobs to those with higher grade averages. But another reason is this: the same habits and skills that make for school success also bring success later on. So when studying gets a little tough, just remember that learning not only benefits you now, but will help you all through life.

Importance of Grades

If you have any plans to go to graduate school, don't neglect your grades *now*. When you apply for graduate study, you can be sure that your grades will be examined very carefully, because, as mentioned above, experience has proved that good grades are the best predictors of success. Registrars follow this rule, "Those who have made good grades in the past will also make them in the future."

Today colleges and graduate schools can be choosy about the students they admit. The supply does not match the demand. Our institutions of higher learning are bulging at the "semesters" with more students than they can accommodate. As a result, they select and keep those who prove themselves by their grades.

2 | You Can Study Less

Everyone likes a shortcut. And the happy thought is that there are short cuts in studying as well as in other things.

A good student may not have any higher I.Q. than his classmate who is a poor student. What makes the big difference? Usually, study habits. Indeed, good study habits are efficient tools that enable you to get more done in less time. From the time that you save, you have more left over for other things you would like to do. You are able to engage in more social and extra-curricular activities. Or, if you're paying your way through school, you will have more time for outside work.

Research has shown this: in many different schools and universities, students who have been trained in how-to-study methods made, on the average, better grades than other students who spent *more* time in studying. So, it isn't *how much* you study; it's *how well* you study that counts. In one school, when students were divided into groups according to how much they studied, it turned out that those who studied a great deal actually made poorer grades than those who studied less. This wasn't necessarily because they had poor academic ability. Many of the students were relatively bright and studied day and night, yet for some reason, they did not get top grades. The major factor was the *quality* rather than the *quantity* of study time. The fact is, most of us could do more in less time if we only learned how. So if you want to study less, learn to study well.

3 | Where to Study

Every outstanding student knows that his success depends, in part, on finding the right place to study. He realizes that his study environment determines not only how fast, but also how well he learns. The location sets the climate for the quality of work he is able to do.

Finding a good place to study seems like a rather easy task. But more than one student has learned that it is not quite that simple. You not only need a *place* that is suitable; you must guard against those who might *interrupt*.

Some students are fortunate to have a quiet room to themselves in a private home. But others must share a place with one or more roommates. Still others use the facilities of the school itself, or study regularly in the library. But whatever the case, you can make the best of your situation. Take the case of Mr. Smith who was working toward his doctorate. He was upset because he did not have a very likely place to do his work. After listening to him for a few minutes, his major advisor said, "I know it's a problem, but most of the men who have earned their doctor's degree at this university have done so under unfavorable conditions."

Even if you do not have an ideal place to study, you can overcome the handicap. You know, of course, that people are creatures of habit. They respond to regular patterns. It is best, then, to have a *regular* time to study and a familiar place. Changing locations does not usually bring good results. If you have trouble with people *interfering*, realize that nothing just now is more important to you than study. Then make it known that you do not want to be disturbed. Your *intelligent* friends will admire you for it.

Naturally, a *clean desk* is a better place to work than a desk cluttered with souvenirs, mementos, and pictures. In addition to giving you more space, a clean desk eliminates influences that too easily set you to daydreaming and wasting your time. If your desk or table is located at "42nd Street and Broadway," try to turn it around so that you do not notice the traffic.

Adequate *lighting* is also important. When you have plenty of light, you are not only more comfortable, but your

motivation will improve and studying will become a joy rather than a chore.

Watch your *posture* too. You may want to get up once in a while for a stretch. But lying down on the job, as on a bed or the floor, usually inspires sleep, not concentration. It's all right once in awhile, but for the most part, your mind is more alert when you sit in an upright, comfortable position.

4 | A Schedule Saves Time

The first step to successful study is the budgeting of your time. A well-planned schedule in any activity seems to actually make more minutes in a day. This is especially true when studying. A schedule keeps you from vacillating about what to do next. It sees to it that you are doing the right thing at the right time. It eliminates waste motion in "getting ready" to study. It also gives you an incentive to get the job done in the allotted time. If properly managed, it assigns time where time is due, and keeps you from studying something more than it requires, allowing you time where you really need it. With your hours thus organized, you will get the job done quicker and find that you actually have more time, not only for study, but for play!

When to Study

A good way to plan a study schedule is to apportion your time to specific subjects, not just for "study." This will save you time deciding what to do and will help you make sure that you have the right materials at hand. (Not being ready to study is one of the most common time consumers.) By scheduling time for studying specific subjects, you can do your work in each as it needs to be done. Otherwise, it is easy to find yourself behind, cramming on one subject, or working too far ahead on another.

Certain things should be studied at particular times and not at others. It is often helpful to allot a period of study close to the class period of that particular subject. If the class time is devoted mostly to lecture rather than recitation, a study period immediately *after* class may be advisable. On the other hand, if class time is largely spent in recitation, try to schedule a period of review just *before* class.

Making and Revising Your Schedule

Study schedules are not static. You plan a time budget realizing that it is subject to change. You make one, then revise it in the light of your experiences. In any case, the schedule is to serve *you* and it must fit your individual needs.

In summary, follow these guides as you plan your schedule:
1. Schedule your study for the time when you work best, not when your energy is at low ebb.
2. Have a definite period of study time reserved for each subject.
3. Tackle the difficult subjects when you are freshest.
4. Vary your type of subjects, do not put together two like subjects.
5. Set up your study periods so that each one is of moderate length. A very brief time of rest should separate each period. For example, you might set up ½ to 1 hour study periods with 5-10 minute "breaks" or rest periods.
6. Don't schedule yourself so that you have to work too fast.
7. Plan your recreation, exercise, social activities, and devotional time as carefully as you do your study hours.

WEEKLY SCHEDULE

HOURS A.M.	Mon.	Tues.	Wed.	Thurs.	Fri.	Sat.	Sun.
6-7							
7-8							
8-9							
9-10							
10-11							
11-12							
P.M.							
12-1							
1-2							
2-3							
3-4							
4-5							
5-6							
6-7							
7-8							
8-9							
9-10							
10-11							

Note: You may want to use half-hours instead of hours or you may want to divide your school hours according to the time of each period.

5 | Briefing For Study

1. If possible, get the dictionaries, texts, and reference books you will need. This will eliminate unnecessary breaks and delays.

2. Select a place to study where it is quiet, and if possible, where you can continue to study each day. Like all others, you will respond to a routine — same place, same time.

3. Protect yourself from interruptions. People, phones, radios, and television — these and many others will cheat you out of precious study time if you do not set up safeguards.

4. The most important and hardest part is getting started. This simply requires self-discipline. Don't wait for inspiration. Start immediately. The inspiration will come after you get going.

5. Study as rapidly as possible, and yet be thorough. Be sure of your work, then keep going.

6. Develop a regular study routine. This will help you to learn faster and better. It will also save you time.

7. Relax now and then. After a period of study, get up from your desk. A stretch and some fresh air will give you new alertness and enthusiasm.

8. Observe good health habits so that you feel physically fit. Such things as over-eating and under-sleeping will keep you from being your best.

9. Alternate your different types of study activities. For example, do some reading, then writing, or solve mathematics problems, then memorize, then read, then draw.

10. Keep spiritually in tune by reading God's Word, praying, and associating with Christian friends.

6 | The Mystery of SQ3R

What are the secrets for studying? Some years ago at Ohio State University, a program was set up to analyze and treat students' academic problems. As a result, the elements of study were condensed into this formula: SQ3R. Since that time, many students around the world have used this approach and have found it works.

Survey

The first of the five steps in studying is the "S," which simply means *survey*. This indicates that you should get the best possible over-all picture of what you are about to study before you study it in any detail. Before you can understand and make intelligent decisions concerning the details, you must see the general picture.

There are several suggested steps in surveying most text books. When you first pick up a book, read the preface. Here the author quickly gives you an idea of why he wrote the book and what he will attempt to do in it. By reading the preface, you can learn what kind of book it is and for whom it is intended. In any case, the preface usually gives some picture of what is to follow.

Next, turn to the table of contents. Scan it thoughtfully, noting the contents and their order.

Now, leaf through the book, reading the chapter summaries. In a short time, you can turn every page of an average textbook, glancing at the headings and reading occasional sentences under them. This procedure is valuable since it gives you a feel for the book and an understanding of its over-all organization. This bird's eye view is essential.

Authors usually organize their words under various headings. This is done so that the reader can know what to expect as he reads. Most textbooks have a heading on nearly every page. Note the order of the headings. Often the arrangement indicates what topics are subordinate to the main ones. It is wise to observe some of the pictures and charts. They tell a quick story, too.

Question

The "Q" in SQ3R represents *question,* and it emphasizes the importance of asking questions for learning. People usually remember what they learn in answer to questions better than things which they have read or memorized. Asking questions gives a *purpose* to learning. Answers to our own questions make an impression on us. They make whatever we are studying more meaningful.

You should raise questions like these when you survey a chapter. "What is the main topic? How does the author substantiate his point of view? What specific answers does this furnish me? How can I use this information in class or in a report?" Eventually the art of asking questions becomes very natural as you read material. This will bring focus to your study and it will cause your learning to stay with you longer.

Read

The first "R" of SQ3R stands for *read*. Notice that this does not come first. Reading should follow your survey and questions. Reading is not necessarily the most important part of studying. This is only the detailed approach after you have surveyed the area and have raised questions. There are many ways to read, different things to look for, and different speeds at which to read. Which way you read depends on your purpose. In fact, in studying assignments, you should "read" the same material several times, each time with a different purpose.

• *Getting the Main Idea.* One purpose in reading is to get the main idea. This is the first stage of study. In doing this, you scan headings and skim sentences to give you the main topics and ideas of the chapter. Unless you pick out the essentials, nothing else will be meaningful.

• *Read Actively.* When reading for study purposes, *read actively.* Seek to find the answers — to things you do not understand or to the questions in an assignment. Keep reminding yourself of your job: to understand and remember what you have read.

• *Note Important Terms.* Give special attention to words or phrases that are italicized. They are used, like headings, to emphasize their importance. These are a warning to stop, look, and listen. Repeat these terms to yourself frequently.

• *Note Tables and Other Art Illustrations.* Note tables, graphs, and other illustrations. These often do the job better than words. An illustration may tell an entire story. Sometimes it even carries a meaning which is expressed in no other way. The old saying, "A picture is worth a thousand words" may be especially true of tables, charts, and graphs.

- *Evaluation.* Another purpose in reading is evaluation. This is especially true of controversial materials. For example, a newspaper or a magazine article may be strongly colored by the personal bias of the author, especially when he is a non-Christian. So evaluate as you read; it is important.

Compare what the book says with what you know and believe. Ask yourself why the author goes against your views. What is his evidence? This is one way of keeping alert, of picking out main ideas and important details, and of evaluating them. In this way, you will learn to *judge* for yourself rather than merely soaking up what an author has said.

Recite

The second "R" in SQ3R represents *recite*. Recitation is an excellent way to learn. In a sense, it is a "testing" method. It is a good way to find out what you actually remember.

While reading, stop at intervals to recite the main points of each major section. When reviewing for examinations, bring recitation into action. It will help you "permatize" what you have learned.

Recitation also assists in other ways. It helps you focus on your reading. You can't daydream while you are recalling facts and saying them aloud. Recitation also permits correction of mistakes. It shows where you have misunderstood the content.

Review

The last "R" in SQ3R represents *review*. A review is actually a survey, except that it is in a follow-up position. When you review the headings of the book, you can ask yourself what they mean and what they contain. Under each, you can note the points you have read and want to remember.

After you have followed the first four steps of SQ3R, review will be easy. The first review is best if it follows immediately after you have studied something. For example, after you have read a chapter, go back and review it. Try to

recite the important points. Also read your notes and recite them to yourself. This first review may be fairly brief, for there has been little time for forgetting. It is wise to have one or two reviews between the first and the final ones for an examination.

The final review, just before an examination, should emphasize recitation. Review *all* the material. Budget your time so you can cover it completely. Naturally, reviewing should not be crammed into the last few hours before a test. This makes the job too hard, and it never gives you the mastery you could have with a few well-spaced reviews.

These, then, are the five steps in SQ3R: Survey, Question, Read, Recite, and Review. They have been tried by thousands of students. Those who have learned and applied them have improved their grades and have found satisfaction in study that they never knew before. *You can too!*

7 | Increasing Your Reading Skill

Someone has estimated that you get at least 50% of your knowledge from reading. If this is true, your reading skill is very important. Poor reading habits can cause study difficulties, poor marks, and even failure. If you can read (and understand) 400 words a minute, you have to spend only about half as much time in reading as the student who reads only 200 words per minute.

The Reading Process

When a person reads, his eyes go across a line of print from left to right in short movements. They stop or pause from time to time and move ahead. During these stops, or "fixations" as they are called, he does his reading. When he comes to the end of the line, his eyes take a long jump back to the left end of the next line.

The eyes of a skillful reader jump rhythmically and evenly across a line. The number of times they stop on each line are about the same. Their pause at each stop or "fixation" is about the same length. The same number of words is usually "taken in" at each stop by the eyes. Poor reading ability may be caused by the way a person reads. He may make too many stops across a line or pause too long at each stop. His eyes may jump backwards frequently in order to go back over something already read, which only causes delay as well as interruption of train of thought. He may not "hit" the beginning of the next line. Or, he may take in too few words at each stop.

Reading for Various Purposes

A teacher once raised this question: "What are the various ways of reading?" Most of the class didn't understand the question. Actually there *are* various ways of reading. The good reader varies his rate depending upon his purpose in reading and the difficulty of the material to be read. His reading rate is fast if reading material is easy or familiar, if he is only refreshing his memory, or if he is just looking for main ideas, not details. On the other hand, he reads at an average rate of speed, or his reading rate is normal, if he is reading for details. But when he is following directions, or analyzing, or when material is complicated, his reading rate is slow.

The good reader reads the fastest when he is skimming. This usually precedes careful reading. You swiftly survey the material to be read by running your eyes down a page or through a chapter. Of course, this does not take the place of detailed reading. But there is a definite place for skimming. You may skim to:
- Get an overall picture of the contents or main ideas.
- Locate specific information.
- Discover the author's style.
- Decide if a book has what you want.
- Refresh your memory.

Vocalizing

A good reader does not vocalize as he reads — that is, he doesn't move his lips, tongue, or throat muscles. These unnecessary movements would slow him down because his eyes move much faster than his vocal muscles pronounce. Reading at a talking rate is slow. Ordinary speech is at a rate of about 100 to 125 words a minute. Good readers should read from 200 to 600 words a minute, depending on the material. But you can't make this speed moving your lips. So check on yourself; push yourself to a speed beyond that of lip moving.

A skillful reader reads by phrases or by a series of words rather than by individual words — that is, he mentally groups the words of a sentence into thought units or phrases and reads them, rather than reading each word separately.

Comprehension

Naturally, the most important element in reading is comprehension. This is a mark of a good reader. He understands well what he reads. Good reading comprehension depends upon:
- A satisfactory reading rate.
- Reading without moving lips, tongue, or throat muscles.
- Concentration while reading.
- Adequate vocabulary.
- A questioning or evaluating attitude.
- General experience and knowledge.

Your Vocabulary

All outstanding readers give attention to vocabulary. This helps them in reading because they perceive the meaning of words at a glance, without thinking. It also helps them in lecture periods because they comprehend what is said. So, an important part in learning how to study is to learn the meaning of words.

You can build a good vocabulary by looking and listening for new words. When you see a new word or one that is not very familiar, don't just skip it; look it up in a dictionary. In brief, get the *dictionary habit*. Keep a dictionary handy at all times when you study.

For courses in which you must learn many new terms and definitions, make a list of all new words and phrases you come across. Review them occasionally, then watch your vocabulary grow!

After learning new words, *put them to use*. Write them down on a card or in your notebook. Title your page, "Vocabulary." Keep incorporating these new words in your daily speaking. At the end of the day or some other convenient time, review them.

Some textbooks contain a glossary of terms. Don't overlook it. Outstanding students have various ways of listing and studying new words and terms. They give special attention to this important part of reading and studying.

How to Improve Your Reading Ability

Many students have learned to increase their reading ability. Here are some ways to improve your reading skills:
1. Try to read, with good comprehension, more pages than usual in a given length of time.
2. Set up a practice schedule for the week, beginning with easy reading matter. Read at a rapid rate and, as you improve, use more difficult reading material.
3. Focus on the most important words in the line; words around them will be "taken in."
4. Break sentences into phrases or units of thought as you read; read for ideas rather than words.
5. Increase your vocabulary.
6. If possible, attend a school reading clinic for a short time.

8 | Taking and Keeping Notes

One of the important parts of studying concerns taking and keeping notes. Research proves that you remember the things you actively *do* much better than those which you merely hear about. That's why recitation is so valuable. In fact, taking notes is like reciting. Instead of *saying*, you are *writing*.

In addition, taking notes makes reviewing much easier. If, in a reading assignment, you carefully outline a chapter, you can usually condense to three or four pages what covers twenty or thirty in a book. Now you have the meat without the extra words. If your outline is accurate, your review is a simple matter. And since you have written it, you probably do know the material or can quickly relearn it.

Helter-Skelter Notes

Some students grab any pieces of paper that happen to be handy, large or small, lined or unlined, punched or unpunched. After scribbling their notes on such odd bits, they stick them into their book, throw them into a folder, or just let them lie around on the desks. Later on, when an examination comes, they search frantically for their notes. "Oh," they cry, "I've lost my notes!"

Proper Note Taking

A loose-leaf notebook, probably the kind with three rings which permits pages to be quickly shifted around or discarded, is a must. Set up your notebook with dividers, one for each subject, and write the name of each subject on the divider. At the end of the book, keep a good supply of unused ruled paper. Make your notebook a constant companion during your class and study hours.

Label each set of notes. At the top of the page write the date and the topic. For textbook notes, write the number and title of the chapter and the pages. A glance then tells you what the notes are about.

Which Notes?

Guard against taking too many notes. A textbook copied in longhand or a lecture taken in detail is cluttered with too much wordage to be of much value. So learn to cull out the salient points, then write them down in brief, but understandable form.

Write legibly. Even people who normally have a good hand are sometimes in such a hurry when taking notes that they write sloppily. Later they find it impossible to make out their own scrawl. There is no advantage in hurrying at the sacrifice of legibility. Legible notes are so valuable to you later that the time you take to make them is fully repaid. Furthermore, it takes just about as long to write poorly as it does to write well. If your writing is hard to read anyway, make a special effort to improve it when you take textbook notes.

Pushing a pen is often easier than pulling a pencil. Pencil points have a way of getting dull. Also, ink is easier to read. However, if you prefer pencils to pen, it is a minor detail. It is, however, important to be comfortable in the media you use.

Taking lecture notes requires practice. It also takes time and effort after class to *edit* and perhaps to *rewrite* or type the notes. But good lecture notes can be the key to real academic improvement.

Getting the Organization

Notice the organization of the lecture. This is like noting the heading of a chapter. But in a lecture you must often figure out for yourself what the headings are. Have you noticed that some lecturers use the blackboard to write down the main topics? Naturally this is helpful as it provides the skeleton for your notes. When the lecturer does not do this, you must make up or pick out the outline for yourself. At times, however, this is almost impossible and you will have to write down what seems to be important, then organize it after class. Even the most disorganized lecturer, however, gives you many clues to his organization if you will recognize and use them. One clue may be the statement, "The main point is this," or "Note this," or "Remember this." Another clue may be the mere repetition of a statement. If the lecturer takes the trouble to say something twice, he must think it is important. Or he may say essentially the same thing in two or three different ways, which is a form of repetition. Changes of pace may serve as a hint. When a lecturer suddenly slows down and says something as though he especially wanted you to get it, his statement is probably important. If his voice changes in tone or loudness, thus giving the statement emphasis, he is signaling an important point.

The question of how many notes you should take depends on you. It also depends on the lecturer and how many main points he has. Some lecturers pack a lot into an hour, others relatively little. Some students do their best by taking many notes and others do just as well by taking relatively few. In general, though, it is best to be selective.

In summary, observe the following:
1. During a lecture, get "set" to listen. Prepare to hear.
2. Use a large notebook, preferably 8½ x 11 inches. You will be able to add outlines, mimeographed material, typed references, copies of term papers and reports.
3. Date every page and place course name and number at the top.
4. Write legibly, using understandable abbreviations.
5. You will probably want to keep your class notes on the right hand pages, on one side of the paper only, so that you can use the left-hand pages opposite for outlining and making notes from your textbook.
6. Keep the notes for each course together and in order by (a) planning a separate section of your loose-leaf notebook for each set; or (b) by using a separate 8½ x 11 notebook for certain courses. Side-opening, spiral binding notebooks with index tabs have real advantages over other notebooks.
7. Make your notes ABC (accurate, brief, and clear.)

Using Cards

Cards enable you to organize and reorganize your notes in any sequence that suits you. For example, if you are doing library research, you can have one card for each article. Later you can rearrange these cards in any sequence you wish.

Many students find that 4 x 6 cards are the best since they are not too large, yet by using both sides they are large enough. It's important, too, to have a card box in which you can file your cards.

In noting references on a card, list the name or names of the author(s), including all initials given on the title page, the title of the book, the place where it is published, the name of the publisher, and its copyright date.

In general, write brief summaries. What you consider important depends on your purpose in doing the research. If you miss some of the main points the first time you read the article, you have the reference on your card and you can look up the article again. Most of the time, though, a thoughtfully written summary will suit your purpose.

When all your reading is accomplished, you may wish to run through your cards, making rough notes on a sheet of paper. Then, using your rough notes as a key to this outline, you will find it easy to rearrange your cards or subjects so that they are approximately in the order you want them.

9 | Learning to Memorize

A good carpenter is clever with his tools. An artist knows his techniques. This is true of all people who get a job done. And so the top student is skillful in *his* techniques. One of the skills a student uses nearly every day is memorization. And like everything else, this skill can be *learned*, then *improved*.

You can save yourself much time and concern if you give some thought to memorization, then start putting your insight into action. In other words, if you begin now to better your ability to memorize, you will find some improvement almost immediately.

Learning to memorize must follow sound, scientific principles. The following will prove helpful to you:

1. *Learn your material thoroughly.* Memorizing is learning — learning well. The more thoroughly you learn, the longer it stays with you. So when you memorize, be sure that you are not doing it by rote. Come to understand it well, then it will assume a meaningful place in your mind.

2. *Analyze that which you are learning.* One of the best ways to understand a fact is to analyze it. By looking into it carefully, you will see its significance. Ask questions about the material. Open it up and look at it carefully. This will help you retain it longer.

3. *Divide it into manageable parts.* If your material is short, it is usually best to learn it as a whole. But if it is long, divide it into parts which you can manage. For example, if you are learning the First Psalm, read the first three verses, noting that they concern the righteous man. Then read verses 4 and 5, noting that they concern the unrighteous man. Then note that the last verse concerns *both* the righteous man and unrighteous man. When it is divided into parts, it not only has more meaning, but it is short enough to comprehend easily.

4. *Put your material into writing.* If possible, write or type your material. This brings kinesthetic (muscular) learning into play. Since you usually remember best the things you touch, writing will help to "permatize" material in your mind.

5. *Say it aloud.* When you say material aloud, you not only use your vocal chords, but you also hear it with your ears. This gives a double impression. If possible, say it to a friend. This not only gives you a verbal and auditory impression; it connects the material to another person. These impressions will all help.

6. *Associate your material with various facts and conditions.* The more you tie your material in with other things, the more permanent it becomes. These tie-ins may be facts, people, ideas, or a host of other things. For example, if a person is memorizing a short poem from a story, it is well to associate the two in your memory. One will strengthen the other.

7. *Make your material vivid.* Do something to make it stand out and take a prominent place. This will impress it more firmly on your mind. Words, rules, and other things may be written in colored pencil or in large letters. This will give it special consideration and help to keep it fresh.

8. *Space your learning.* Research shows that it is better to break your learning periods into several sections, rather than trying to memorize it all at one time. This is true because the mind seems to absorb and keep on learning after you have stopped your conscious efforts.

9. *Review frequently.* There is much to be learned. And, of course, the human mind is able to absorb and hold only a portion of that which comes to its attention. So review keeps facts alive. This frequent attention to something you have learned revives it to a prominent place so that it takes precedence over less important facts and experiences.

10 | Using the Library

The person who makes good grades is the one who knows how to use the library. He knows what is available and where to look for it. It is easy to learn how to use a library. Here are suggestions that will improve your skills.

Encyclopedias

When you need information on a specialized topic such as imperialism or Greek mythology, it is wise to begin with a good encyclopedia. One of the best-known American encyclopedias is the Encyclopaedia Britannica, but for many purposes, other works such as the Encyclopedia Americana are equally as good or perhaps better. Large libraries stock many encyclopedias. An article in an encyclopedia usually gives an excellent introduction to a topic and sometimes much detail as well. Such articles have well-selected bibliographies, and these make good suggestions for further reading in the field.

Books

There are times when you need specific books on a subject. The best place to look is in the United States Catalog. It lists books by their author, title, and subject. It is kept up to date by its Cumulative Book Index and a regular supplement. If you are looking for an exact citation for a book and know only its author, you will find this source very helpful. It is often a more convenient source of information than a small library or where the card catalog is inconvenient.

How do you look over a book to decide what is in it, how good it is and whether it has what you want? Here are a few points to check:
1. The author — not only his name, but title, background, degree, position, and writings are given on the title page. There are clues to help you judge his qualifications as an authority.
2. The copyright date — one indication of whether the writing is up-to-date.
3. The edition — note whether there have been several editions or revisions since the time the book origi-

nally appeared. A hint to popularity as well as to recency.
4. The preface and the foreword — these few pages in the front of a book tell you why and how the author wrote the book, what the book contains, and what help the author received.
5. The table of contents — the chapter titles and subtitles are an outline of the book.
6. The bibliography — found either at the end of the book or at the end of each chapter or section — lists books, magazine articles, and pamphlets used in preparing the book or those recommended by the author.

Periodicals

When you need an article from a magazine, journal, or an important newspaper, look it up in the Reader's Guide to Periodical Literature and/or the International Index of Periodicals. The Reader's Guide covers articles in popular magazines and less technical journals, while the International Index covers articles in more technical journals in the humanities, arts, and sciences. If you are looking for articles or editorials in newspapers, the monthly New York Times Index is the best source.

Biographical Information

If you are interested in information about well-known people, there is a whole library of biographical reference books available to you. For American statesmen, writers, and other outstanding people who are no longer living, there is the *Dictionary of American Biography*. For current information on such people as congressmen, judges, public officials, writers, and so on, there are the various *Who's Who*. *Who's Who in America* is the most general biographical reference for living Americans. In addition, there are many specialized books such as *Who's Who in Education* or *American Men of Science*, which contain information about people in specific fields.

A Library Classification System

Books are arranged on shelves by classes and books in each class have some further identifying sign. If you understand the system, you can find the books you want.

The most widely used library classification system is the Dewey Decimal System, in which there are ten main classes as illustrated below.

Range of Numbers	Class	Examples of Subjects or Books Included
000-099	General Works	Encyclopedias, indexes, other reference works
100-199	Philosophy	Psychology, conduct, right living
200-299	Religion	Churches, Christianity, books about the Bible
300-399	Social Sciences	Education, economics, government, vocations
400-499	Philology	Grammar, language, linguistics
500-599	Pure Science	Chemistry, physics, mathematics, biology
600-699	Useful Arts	Agriculture, engineering, aeronautics, medicine
700-799	Fine Arts	Painting, music, sculpture
800-899	Literature	Plays, poetry, essays
900-999	History	Geography, travel

Know Your Library

You should know the arrangement or layout of both the school and public libraries. Explore them so that you know various locations. For example, in your own libraries, do you know the location of:

_____the card catalogue?
_____the charging desk?
_____the delivery desk?
_____the reading rooms?
_____the stacks?
_____the reference books?
_____the magazines and newspapers?
_____the reserved books?
_____the special collections of books?
_____the sections for special fields?
_____the open shelves?
_____the desks of library specialists?

11 | Writing Themes and Reports

Since most of your work in school is written, it is especially important that you develop this skill. Many otherwise outstanding students have made poor grades because they did not understand the techniques of writing.

Most of the procedures used for writing a theme or composition may be used in preparing a talk or speech. Here are some valuable tips:

1. Choose your topic (this is not necessarily your title).
2. Write down your ideas on the topic (no special order).
3. Arrange and organize your ideas.
4. Select your temporary title.
5. Make an outline.
6. Write the first draft (double space if typewritten).
7. Revise the rough draft.
8. Read your composition aloud, editing as you go.

Let some time pass, if possible, before you begin revising the rough draft. Then, you can look at your first copy with a more critical and fresher attitude. New ideas may strike you or, at least, better ways of expressing those you have. Weak points are more easily spotted, too. Mark up the first draft all you please. Cross out or insert words and paragraphs to your heart's desire.

If time permits, your procedure may be as follows: first draft, revision of first draft, second draft, revision of second draft, and so on to final copy. Remember: *writing is rewriting!* Check yourself by using the following questions. This will give your masterpiece the professional touch:

1. Does your first paragraph introduce the subject so well that your reader knows what you are going to write about and wants to read more?
2. Is the first or topic sentence of each paragraph strong?
3. Rather than jumping abruptly from one idea to another, do you connect one paragraph with another smoothly?

4. Do all your paragraphs relate to the subject?
5. Are your paragraphs in logical order?
6. Are your words and expressions descriptive, indicative of action, and clear rather than dull, stiff, and vague? Remember to use active verbs!
7. Are most of your sentences under fifteen to twenty words? Long sentences usually become complicated.
8. If appropriate, have you made your composition attractive by giving illustrations, personal experiences or quotations, and by including pictures, cartoons, drawings, or snapshots?
9. Is the concluding paragraph strong, with a summary of your thinking?
10. Would you enjoy reading a composition like yours?

12 | When You Give That Speech

Learning to speak well is one of the most valuable assets a person can have. The one who can stand on his feet and state his thoughts clearly and well is always in demand. Since much of your work in school involves speaking, improving your speaking ability is a must. Do not think of oral assignments as something you should dread. Rather, look forward to them as opportunities to improve your art of communication.

1. *Uneasiness Is Normal.* Do you sometimes feel a little uneasy and nervous when you speak in public? If so, this is proof that you are normal! Speaking usually makes most people a bit nervous — sometimes exceedingly nervous. This is understandable inasmuch as you have to speak alone, you are facing a crowd (some of whom may be rather analytical and critical), and in all possibility you have not had much experience speaking in public. So all of this adds up to nervousness. But the more you learn about speaking and the better you do it, the more your fear will leave you. Then you will enjoy speaking, probably more than almost any other thing. In fact, there are few experiences in life that are more rewarding than learning to stand in front of a group, giving your ideas, and seeing the group follow you intently.

2. *Preparation Brings Confidence.* There is nothing which dispells fear and uneasiness like adequate preparation. If you know what you are going to say and how you are going to say it, you will begin to focus on your subject and your techniques rather than on yourself. So whether you memorize a speech or just carry some notes, make sure that you have adequate preparation. If possible, find an opportunity to say the speech out loud to somebody or some object, perhaps in your room. It is amazing how a little verbal practice before you come to class paves the way for an easy presentation. You may want to go out into the park or yard and quickly run through your speech (trees and

birds make good audiences.) Many students do this and they find that it gives them real confidence.

3. *Selecting a Topic.* Naturally, your first job in preparing a talk is to consider a general topic. This does not mean a title. Rather, it refers to the subject on which you choose to speak. In selecting a topic, ask yourself whether it would interest you if someone else in the class were giving it. In fact, you may want to consider several topics, do a little thinking about each, then select one for your presentation.

4. *Outlining the Topic.* Your next step is to make a brief outline of your topic. This puts your topic to a real test. It will reveal whether the topic can be broken down into several sub-topics and whether it is worthy of using. One of the easiest ways to develop a subject is to use these words: *Who, where, what, why, how,* and *when.* Undoubtedly some of these words will help you develop sub-topics. For example, if you were giving a talk on a recent discovery, you would want to mention *who* was involved. You would also discuss *where* it took place. So use these six pertinent words. They prove successful every day to men who make a living by speaking professionally.

5. *The Introduction.* Your introduction is important because it puts your best foot forward. It captures the attention of your audience. It also gives you confidence. Your best introduction may not come to you until near the end of your preparation — perhaps only a day or so before you give your speech. However, it is wise to develop some kind of introduction rather early in your preparation, even if it is only a straight-forward kind such as, "I have chosen a topic which interests many people. I am sure it interests most of us here today." After you have toyed with several introductions, one will emerge as superior.

6. *Filling in the Outline.* After you have written the basic outline for your speech, you can start filling it in. Each point is sufficiently focused so that you can say what needs to be said quite easily. Some points of your speech deserve considerable expansion. Others may be more brief. But as you rewrite your material, the less-developed sub-points will probably begin to grow.

7. *Rearranging the Outline.* After you have filled in the outline, you will see that some of the major points should be rearranged. For example, point number four may need to come where point number two is. Point number three, on the other hand, may need to be exchanged with point number five. By typing or writing out your speech, or at least making a detailed outline, you can easily see it and know what rearrangement is necessary.

8. *Adding Illustrations.* After you have outlined and filled in the major points of your speech, go back over each one and see where you may insert illustrations. These will make your talk alive. It is one thing, for example, to say that the school had a lot of spirit. It's quite another thing, however, to give an illustration of it. Your illustrations may be from real life or ones which you create to fit the point. They may also come from something you have read or heard about. At any rate, they will add luster and meaningfulness to what you say.

9. *Raising Questions and Resolving Them.* Nearly all outstanding speakers know that at various points in their speech it is good to ask a question, then discuss the answer. This is always arresting, and it is a way of focusing people's attention upon the main points. It also gives drive and motion to your speech.

10. *Using Quotations.* It is easy to dress up your speech by including a few appropriate quotations. This can be easily done by consulting a book of quotations in your library. There you will find scores of quotations on any topic. These important sayings will add weight to what you are saying and they will also give a literary touch which will be greatly appreciated.

11. *Appropriate Scripture.* The final authority in all life is the Bible. God says that His Word is settled in heaven. Of course, nothing will add to your speech as much as quotations from the Word of God. So look over your outline and see where you might include an appropriate verse. This will lift your entire presentation out of the ordinary and give it ultimate authority.

12. *A Touch of Humor.* Everybody likes a laugh now and then. Some topics lend themselves to a touch of humor here and there. It may be, of course, that your topic does

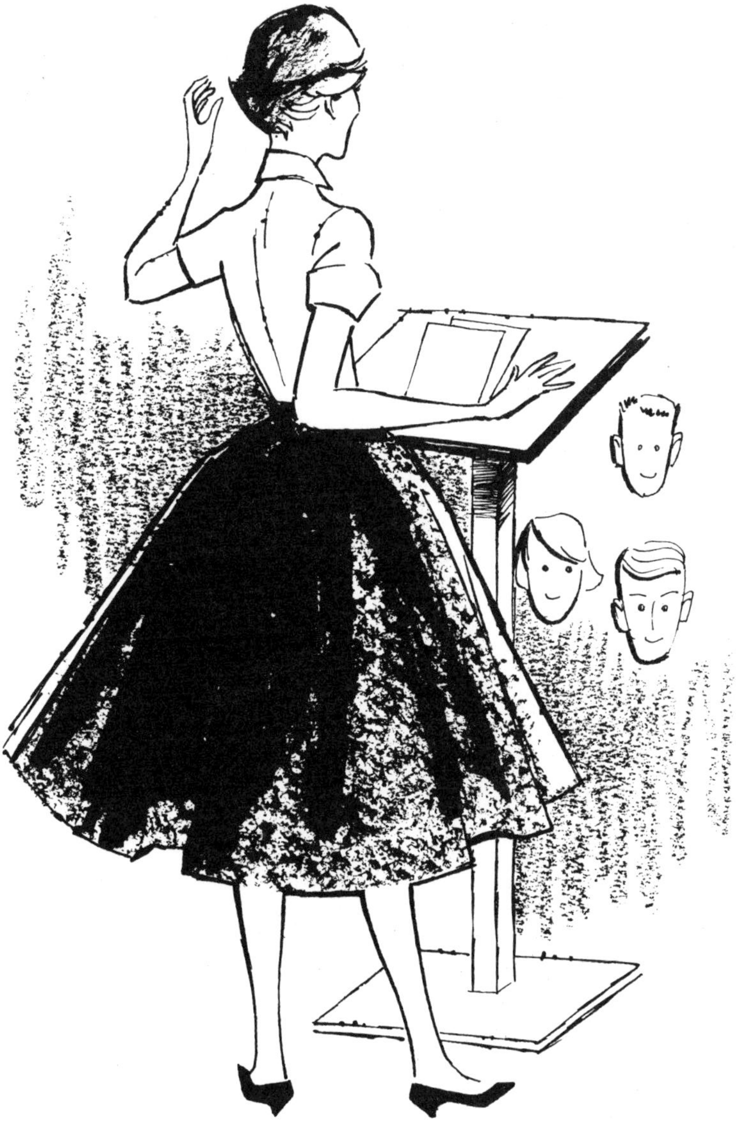

not lend itself to such, but most topics do. So look over your outline and see where you might sprinkle in a clever statement, a humorous quotation, or some other bit of levity that will give your speech a touch of lightness.

13. *Summarizing at the Close.* Most oral presentations are best if they end with a measure of summary. This not only re-emphasizes the major points, but it tells your audience psychologically that the presentation is being brought to a close. The summary points may also lead into a final sentence or so of inspiration, thereby ending your speech with a climax.

14. *Techniques of Speaking.* You have seen, of course, from what we have been discussing, that the most important thing about your speech is the preparation of it. If you have worthwhile material that is beautifully connected, people will listen. However, you must not overlook a few simple techniques of speaking. One of them is to look at your audience. Whether you are reading a quotation or following an outline, it is important that you look up and meet your audience with your eyes. This brings you close to them and gives your speech a personal touch.

It is important, too, that you not only speak distinctly, but also sufficiently loud that everyone can hear you. Nearly everyone can speak distinctly if he will take his time and concentrate on being understood. Speaking loudly involves projection. Think not only of speaking to the person on the first row, but lift your voice enough to reach the twelfth row comfortably. If you will keep this in mind, you will undoubtedly be heard very well.

It usually helps, also, to make simple, natural gestures with your hands. During your speaking, move forward just a step, or perhaps move to one side a little. This not only brings new interest to your listeners, but it also relaxes you.

In summary, the speaking which you will do in school will not only help you now but also throughout life. So follow these suggestions each time you are called upon to speak, and you will find that you will improve greatly.

13 | Preparing for and Taking Examinations

For Ben, examination time was always a hectic time — cramming, memorizing, losing sleep, and frantically searching for the right answers. But it need not have been. He brought this condition on because he had not budgeted his time wisely and had not reviewed his material periodically. The most important rule for taking examinations is, "Be prepared." This means being prepared for the kind and scope of examination you are to take. It means having a thorough mastery of your subject matter and having it well organized. Adequate preparation also means being rested and mentally alert.

The Final Review

If you have studied well all along, preparing for an examination is largely a matter of reviewing your notes, looking over the main ideas that you have underlined in your textbook, and checking yourself on the technical words used in the course. This review should be intensive. It should, however, be a review and not an attempt to learn things that you should have learned earlier. You may be intelligent enough to get by, but you will do much better if you can use this time for review.

If you have a large amount of material to cover and have a great many notes, you will want to make a set of summary notes. This will be your summary of a summary. Now you have something condensed to run over before the examination. If you will say these notes aloud, you will remember them better.

Taking Examinations

Your examinations are ordinarily of two types. *Objective examinations* are of the true-false, yes-no, completion, matching, or multiple-choice type. *Essay-type examinations* are made up of long-answer questions for which you must write out detailed answers in your own words. Here are practical suggestions for improving your results on both types.

Objective Tests

1. Answer the easy questions first. Those that you find more difficult should be checked and passed by. Don't let them bog you down. If you do, you may waste time and later find yourself rushing through other questions, making mistakes. When you are unsure of an answer, put a check mark in the margin next to the question. After you have answered the easy ones, come back to these. Knowing how much time you have left and how many difficult ones there are, you can apportion your time wisely.

2. Ask whether you will be penalized more for wrong answers than for omitted answers. Your instructor will give this information.

3. If wrong answers count the same as omitted ones, answer every question. If you don't know the answer, guess. However, if you are penalized more for errors than for omissions, answer all the questions you know, then guess at those on which there is better than a 50-50 chance you'll be right.

4. When you go back over your paper, change questionable answers only if you have made an obvious mistake in reading the questions the first time. (First guesses are more likely to be correct.)

5. Make sure you know exactly what the instructor wants. If the question contains such qualifying words as *always, usually,* or *seldom,* be sure to take these words into account in answering. If confusing items arise, ask about them — privately.

6. On multiple-choice questions (choosing from among several answers), you can usually eliminate all but two or three immediately. Then make your choice from those remaining. This eliminates trying to keep all the possible answers in mind at once; your answer is more likely to be right.

7. On completion questions (filling in the correct word, definition, or phrase), there is frequently more than one acceptable answer. Unless you are heavily penalized for wrong answers, write something in every blank.

8. Watch out for such words as "almost," "all," "any," "only," and "totally."

Essay Tests

1. Read the directions and questions carefully. If every question has the same value, divide your time by the number of questions. Spend no more than the allotted time on any one question — unless you finish the test before the time is up. If questions are of unequal value, adjust the time accordingly. When not sure of a question, leave space for it and try the next one. You can return to the hard questions later.

2. Read all questions before answering any. If you don't, you may discover that another question asks for information you have already given.

3. If you are asked to describe, list, evaluate, sketch, outline, criticize, or discuss, be sure to do exactly what is asked. The instructor knows what he wants, and your grade depends on your answering the question in the way you were asked to answer it.

4. When you first read a question, important ideas often occur about various points you could make. Note these on scratch paper *immediately,* and refer to them when you come to the proper place in the test.

5. Organize the answers to a question before you write them. As you organize them in the proper order, you will usually think of several points you want to make clear. Think before — and while — you write. You'll save time, space, words, and worry, and your answers will be clearer.

6. Long answers usually earn better grades than brief ones. In other words, complete answers are better than incomplete ones. Most statements can be elaborated upon by explaining them in several ways and by giving an illustration.

7. If the information you give in answering one question ties up with something in another question, call attention to that fact. It's information about the course, too, and is worth points.

Any Test

1. If you don't know what kind of test you will have, study as though you were going to have an essay test.

2. Don't spend all your time during exam week on reviewing. Have a good time, too. You need some recreation in order to function efficiently.

3. Keep yourself in good physical and mental condition during examination week. Get enough sleep.

4. Reread your paper before you hand it in; make corrections, additions, and any changes you find necessary. This will sharpen and clarify your answers.

5. Remember that it's not only what you know that earns your grades; it's what you let the instructor know that you know.

Finishing the Examination

Leave some time for a final rereading of your examination. Before you turn it in, you should read it through again carefully just in case you have made any mistakes or left any questions unanswered.

When you reread your examination, you may be tempted to change some of your answers. If you feel strongly that an answer should be changed, change it. On the other hand, if you waver between two answers, not being able to make up your mind, don't change your original answer. Research has shown that your first guess, based on a careful reading, is likely to be your best one. If you change an answer when you are quite unsure of yourself, the chances are that it will be wrong.

14 | Impressing Your Teacher

Some students forget that teachers are people, too, and that they want to be treated like human beings. Strangely enough, teachers are sometimes put in a special category that is just a little less than human — insensitive to normal responses. But teachers are not only people, they have a special interest in people; otherwise they would not be teaching. So you will be wise to try to understand and cooperate with them. The better you come to know your teachers and their special characteristics, the easier it will be for you to work closely with them and to meet their requirements.

Since *first impressions* are often lasting ones, it is especially important that you extend yourself toward your teachers during the first few months. Since teachers are human, they tend to form an image of you and then carry that same image around throughout the semester or year. In view of this, it is important that as you enter a new class you help your teacher form the best image possible of you. Is this polishing the apple? Indeed not. It is simply understanding people and working with them in an intelligent, Christian manner.

Probably nothing will impress your teacher as much as your *sincerity*. Most teachers have worked with hundreds of students and they can spot a bluffer a mile off. Consequently, it pays to be sincere! Each day as you have your devotions, ask the Lord to make you honest with yourself and others. As you may know, the word "sincere" means "without wax." It was originally used by sculptors to denote the fact they had not made mistakes and then filled in their mistakes with bits of wax. Be certain that your own life is a true testimony. Your teacher will soon sense this and respect you for it.

Another way to impress your teacher is to hand in *neat work*. If you can type, do so. You can imagine that a teacher who looks over several hundred papers may naturally resent those which are difficult to read. So make the necessary effort to present all of your work in a neat fashion.

Another important classroom procedure is to *carefully listen to instructions,* then carry them out. Learn your teacher's way of doing things and then conform to it. This will not only help you to get along better with that individual teacher, but will make you a more acceptable person to everyone else.

Answering in class is also important. In other words, if you know something, say it. Although some teachers seem to have a fifth sense, they cannot tell whether you know a fact unless you say it or write it. So do not neglect to speak up in class. It is a signal to your teacher that you not only have interest but also information.

If you feel that you need it, do not hestitate to *ask for special help.* A teacher generally appreciates a student who makes special inquiry about assignments. He is interested in you and he appreciates your singling him out and getting individual assistance. A teacher would much prefer giving you some individual assistance than to have you do poor work.

Finally, give your teacher the *recognition* he deserves. You may or may not agree with all he says or does. But you can still respect the fact that he is a faculty member chosen for his special training and competence. So think twice before you say or write things that are offensive or derogatory. An honest disagreement? Of course. You can differ with your teacher in a pleasant way without being offensive. And do not forget the compliments. They always fall on ready ears. When you appreciate your teacher, the chances are he will appreciate you.

These, then, are suggestions for getting along well with teachers. If you review them carefully, you will see that you can use them during your entire life. They work just as well with others as they do with teachers!

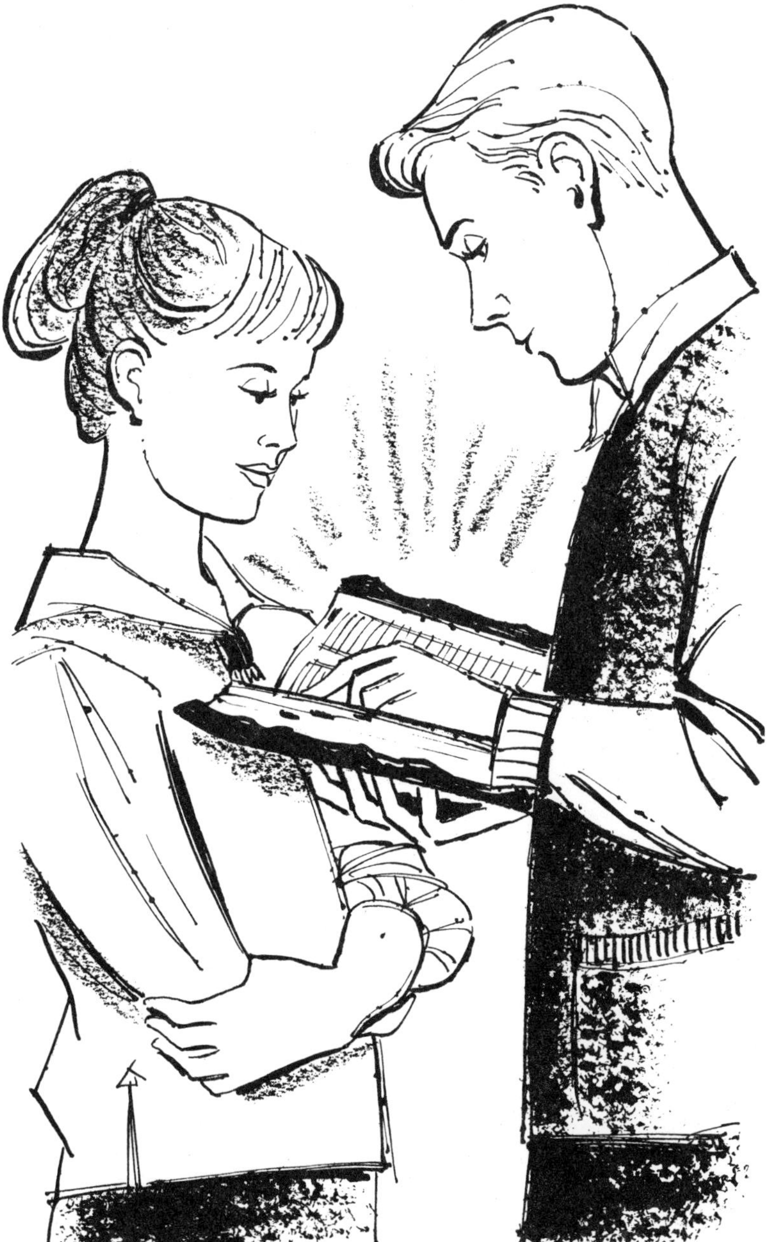

15 | What About Your S.Q.?

We have all heard about the I.Q., but something which is more important is your S.Q. This is your *Spiritual Quotient*. Your S.Q. indicates your relationship to God. God — using *you*, and your relying on Him. This seriously affects your success in school.

There is one major difference between I.Q. and S.Q.: your I.Q. is fairly stable, but your S.Q. may fluctuate a great deal. Sometimes your spiritual life is riding on the crest of the wave, but other times, when you neglect it, Satan hinders your relationship to Christ, thus sending your S.Q. down low.

How does a person keep his S.Q. up? There are several ways. First, be sure you know Christ as your personal Saviour. This is the beginning of spiritual reality. A person's S.Q. is a minus quantity before he is saved. Trying to live the Christian life without belonging to the Lord is like watering a flower pot without any seed in it. You can water today, tomorrow, and all year—yet nothing comes up. Why? Because the seed has not been planted. The same is true in your spiritual life. Until you have been born again, there is no foundation for spiritual growth.

How can you be sure you are saved? The answer is in the Bible. "For whosoever shall call upon the name of the Lord shall be saved" (Romans 10:13). This means that you acknowledge your need. You know you are sinful. Knowing that Christ has died on the cross to save sinners, you ask Christ to come into your heart and save you. The moment you do this, you become a child of God. "But as many as received Him, to them gave He power to become the sons of God, even to them that believe on His name" (John 1:12). If you have not already done this, or are not *sure* whether you have, you can do it *now*. Eternal life is available to you at this very moment. It is God's gift to those who will receive it. "And I give unto them eternal life; and they shall never perish, neither shall any man pluck them out of my hand" (John 10:28).

When you have trusted in Christ as your Saviour, you can keep your S.Q. up by making Him Lord of your life. We draw close to the Lord as we: (1) Study God's Word, (2) Pray every day, (3) Worship regularly, (4) Witness to others, (5) Fellowship with others who know Christ intimately. If you are sincere about walking in fellowship with God, first be certain that you are saved, then check yourself with the above five points every day.

When you follow these basics, your spiritual life will reach new heights. When your sins are forgiven, you have a sense of joy and satisfaction. Now that you are set free from feelings of guilt and confusion, a new harmony is realized in Christ as Saviour. Your outlook on life is changed and your mind is free to focus on study. Like a phonograph record which is carefully centered on the spindle, so your life is centered in Christ. Your study habits will improve because you are now at peace with God and with man. You are now working to "show yourself approved unto God." Life has new purpose and meaning. This results in new energy and confidence. Indeed, being in tune with God does improve your study skills. Thousands of students have proved it to be so. You can prove it too!

THE LIFE GUIDE SERIES: Volume 5

SECTION II:

Improving Your Self-Confidence

Improving Your Self-Confidence

"How can I gain more self-confidence?"

This is a question that has plagued thousands of intelligent people from the beginning of time. "I don't know what my trouble is," they complain, "but other people with much less ability than I push right past me and take the important posts while I am left with a back seat."

Wasted manpower . . . personal frustration . . . unhappiness. How pathetic to see people who *could* make a real contribution, if they had more of the ingredient called self-confidence!

Shy people actually suffer. They do not always hang in the shadows because they dislike the limelight. Many are capable of becoming leaders, but the reason they avoid prominence is because they are fearful and insecure.

"I would like to do something for the Lord," said one woman, "but I'm just too afraid to talk to people. I know that many of my neighbors are not Christians, yet I become petrified when I think of speaking to them about Christ. Even at our Wednesday night prayer and Bible study at church I am too frightened to ask questions. I'm a high school graduate and I have had two years of college. I have time that I would like to use for the Lord, but I can't seem to overcome my self-consciousness."

A young man in training to become the manager of a department store had the same problem. Each member of the training class was required to give a four-minute speech about his department. "I know my department well," he told a friend ruefully, "but I had to go to that class and read my speech because I was scared to death to get up in front of everybody. All the other men got up with their neat little note cards and talked without any trouble. Yet, I know the procedures as well as any of them and could have talked for forty-five minutes on any phase of the operation."

The fearful discomfort of self-consciousness is not limited to adults. A rather shy teen-aged boy once entered a contest to be a songleader for his high school. He learned the motions and had a good sense of rhythm. Yet, when the day came for the contestants to appear before the student body, the boy became so nauseated from sheer fear that he could not go on. Consequently he lost his chance to do what he so desperately wanted and needed to do.

A runner who feels certain that he can jump the hurdles will probably clear them with ease. But the runner who feels unsure of himself will probably come crashing down with the very first one.

It is much the same in music. If a singer is confident that he can sing a high note, he probably will have no trouble reaching it. But if he is afraid that he will miss it, his throat will tighten and his voice will crack.

Even though people have different temperaments, no one is born with confidence. It is something that is developed — and it can be yours!

1 | Competence and Confidence

An interesting story is told about the heroic flyer of World War I, Eddie Rickenbacker. In those days, machine guns on aircraft often jammed and became useless during dogfights in the sky. So each night while his fellow pilots slept, Rickenbacker carefully inserted each bullet in the magazine of his machine gun to make sure it fit perfectly. When he came to a bullet that was imperfect or not altogether round, he would discard it. The next day when his plane flew into the thick of battle, he knew that when he pressed the trigger, his gun would fire accurately and flawlessly.

That is confidence born of experience, confidence which grows out of competence. Any job done well brings a certain measure of confidence. Confidence makes any task a joyful one. Lack of it can make even the smallest duty difficult and unappealing. Indeed, competence and confidence go hand-in-hand. If you can do things well, you know it. Then, of course, you feel confident. People who are incompetent realize their lack, and consequently they do *not* have confidence.

Do you want to increase your self-confidence? Then develop your skills. Typing, cooking, gardening, music, or salesmanship — whatever you already do or aspire to do, learn carefully and strive to excel. There is an old saying, "If a job is worth doing, it is worth doing well."

Obviously, we are not all endowed with the same innate abilities, but we can all be skillful in some area — night schools, day schools, institutes, home study courses — these all exist to help you improve yourself.

One day a young woman casually thumbed through a Christian magazine. She loved the Lord and was eager to be of service to Him, but shyness prevented her from doing what she would like to do. Suddenly her eyes caught an advertisement in the magazine about a Bible correspondence course. She had never attended a Christian college or Bible

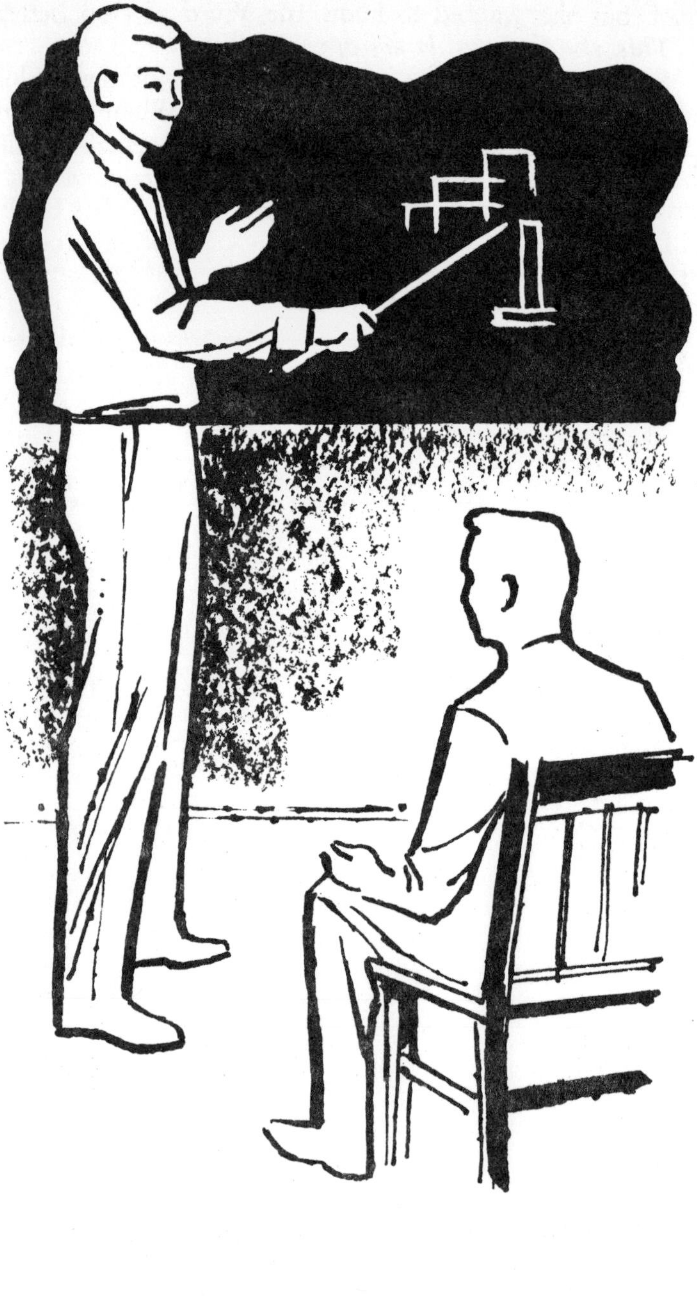

school, but she wanted to know the Word of God better. *This,* she thought, *is my opportunity.*

So she enrolled for a course, "A Survey of the Bible." As months passed, she kept working away. When she completed the course, she began another, "Basic Doctrines of the Bible." Little by little she increased her knowledge of God's Word. In a sense, she was stepping out ahead of her family and friends. She discovered that as her knowledge increased and she began to utilize what she had learned, her shyness tended to disappear.

Before this time, she had been uncertain about the Scriptures. Now she was filled with knowledge of them and could not remain silent! In addition to the knowledge gained, the Holy Spirit had worked in her heart and had given her more self-assurance through Christ.

Indeed, competence is the springboard to confidence. It is basic to the development of poise and it increases your ability to relate well to others. On competence hinges self-assurance. It is the first step toward confidence.

2 | Feeling at Ease

People who are self-confident are usually well poised. They are not concerned about pulling boners because they are reasonably well versed in the knowledge of basic social courtesies.

Good manners usually center around the idea of being thoughtful of others and using discretion in what one says. Today no one needs to be at sea about what is proper and acceptable. There are many books available to help one sharpen up on his "do's" and "don'ts."

A common complaint of diffident people is that they are too self-conscious to make new friends or to mix with others. One of the best ways to conquer a feeling of social inadequacy is to be secure in the knowledge of acceptable behavior. When you know what is customary and proper and when you feel sure of yourself, you will not be unduly concerned about making a social blunder.

Remember that no one is perfect, and people do not expect you to be perfect, either. There are times when all of us make mistakes and find ourselves in embarrassing situations. Such experiences are the real test of poise. It is not nearly as important to do things correctly all the time as it is to take things in stride when unexpected situations arise. When you learn to smile at your own predicaments, you will not only put yourself at ease, but others, too. Marie, for instance, found this difficult because she was raised in a family where mistakes were not permitted. As a child she was always reprimanded for any little thing she did wrong. For her, life was a series of scoldings and lectures. Now as an adult she finds it difficult to break the pattern. Quite unconsciously, she is ill at ease in the fear that she might do something that is not accepted. Consequently, she is self-conscious and shy.

Is there any help for Marie? Yes! The first step in overcoming her difficulty is to recognize what has caused her to be like this. As she thinks and talks it through, she will realize that others do not expect the same perfection of her that her parents did. When she becomes less concerned about making a possible error, she will be able to reach out to others rather than draw into herself for fear she might do something wrong.

You can also improve your social ease by taking inventory of your personal appearance. An ancient Roman leader made the statement, "A good exterior is a silent recommendation." This is very true. Actually, a person does not need to be good looking to make a good appearance. There is a Chinese proverb that says, "Three tenths of a good appearance is due to nature; seven tenths to dress." Although clothes do not "make the man," they do help to make the man and the woman look better. There is no substitute for dressing neatly and appropriately.

When you look right, you feel right. But when you do not, you lose self-confidence. Why? Because inappropriate dress keeps you thinking about yourself. It ties you to yourself rather than to others. So if you are to gain more self-confidence, you must be free to invest yourself in your friends.

This, then, is how to feel at ease with others. First, be sure that you know what is correct and what is expected of you. Always look your best: dress neatly and appropriately. This will give you the assurance that you can do things

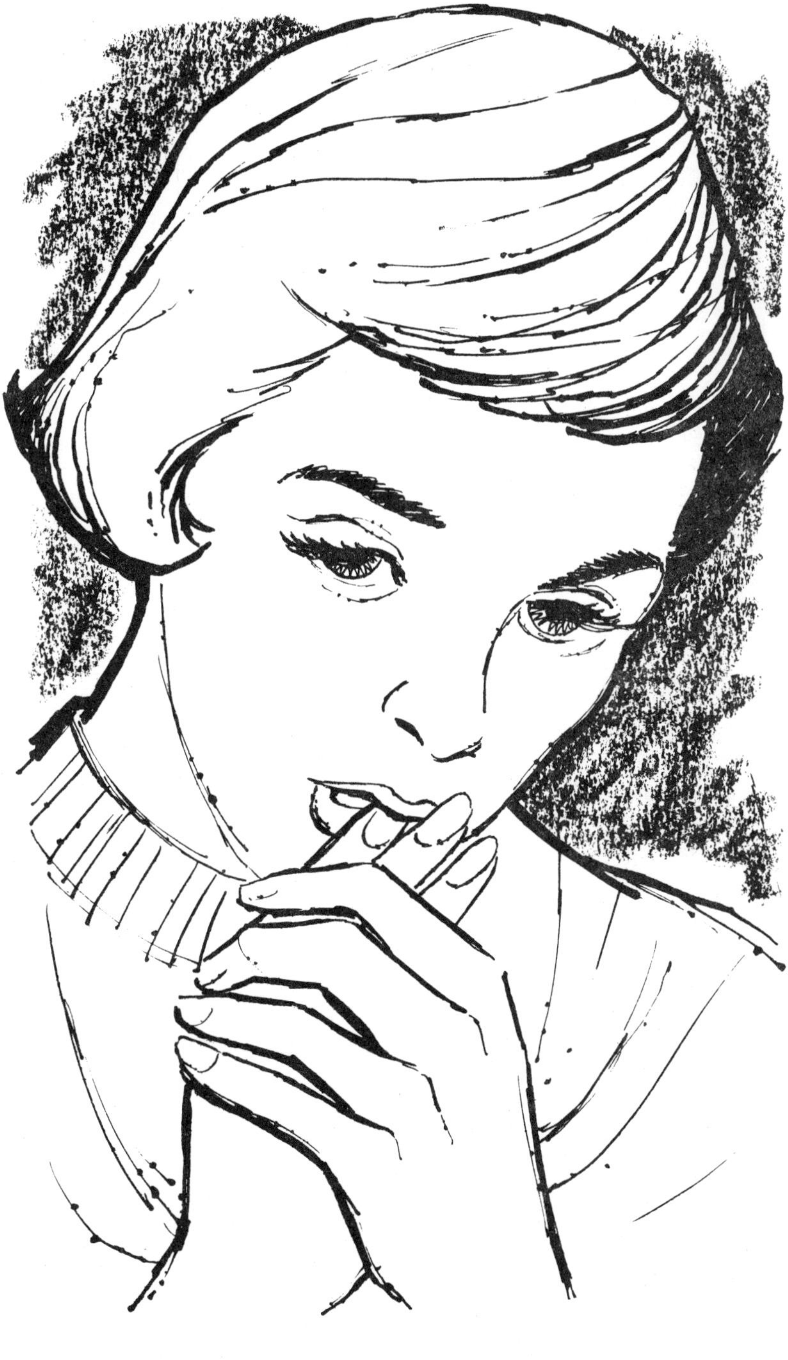

right and that you look right. You will not be under a cloud of uncertainty, wondering if you are about to make a social *faux pas*. Then, after you have learned what is proper, do the best you can, but don't be overly concerned about making an error. If you can learn to glide over mistakes graciously, people will usually forget your errors and think of you as a well poised, confident person.

3 | Conversational Skills

The age-old proverb, "Silence is golden," certainly does not apply to people who are shy. For them the opposite is true. Those who are reticent and retiring must learn to project themselves in conversation and express their thoughts and emotions through speech.

Words are called "tools" of speech. One of the first rules in conversation is to listen attentively to the person with whom you are talking. The fluent speaker does not necessarily make the best conversationalist. Sometimes a shy person is concerned because he does not think he is a good talker. However, a good listener is always in demand. One workable technique in conversation is to ask the other person questions that focus on his ideas and interests. He will love you for it and you will learn much, too.

Here are a few suggestions which will help you improve your conversational skills:

Show a Genuine Interest in Others

Try to remember the names of people you meet. Everyone likes to hear his own name. And if you can recall a person's name, you will make a lasting and favorable impression.

Be Well Informed

When you have a reasonable knowledge of a variety of subjects, you can contribute to almost any conversation. When you have something interesting to say, people are anxious to hear you.

Being well read does not necessarily call for a college degree. It does, however, mean keeping your ears tuned to the times and having a fair understanding of local and world affairs. When you have a reservoir of information from which to draw, it is easy to enter into conversations. You have something worthwhile to say, and you know it. This will give you an added measure of self-assurance.

Don't Take It Personally

You should not be offended if another person does not seem interested in what you have to say. In all possibility, if you know what you are talking about and can express yourself reasonably well, the other person is just a poor conversationalist and has never learned the art of listening. This is no discredit to you. It simply means that he lacks skill in communicating with others.

Keep in mind that unfavorable remarks are, in all probability, not directed toward you. Many people are thoughtless in the things they say. Often their comments are simply the expression of general ideas, and are not aimed at anyone in particular. People who are not shy are not always aware of how their uninhibited statements may affect their sensitive friends. So bury your oversensitive feelings and dismiss the thought that you are the butt of unkind remarks. Learn to give people the benefit of the doubt and avoid taking every statement as a personal assault. This will avert much misunderstanding and you will be a happier, more confident person.

People Are Interested in What You Have to Say

Sometimes a shy person thinks that others are not interested in what he might add to a conversation. This, however, is not true. Naturally, someone who dominates a conversation will undoubtedly receive more attention than you, because it is only human to listen to the one who makes the most noise. In addition, people may not expect you to say anything because you seldom do. However, what you *do* say may carry more weight than the expressions of your loquatious friends. People know that you do more thinking than talking — thus your ideas are respected and welcomed. So remember, people *are* interested in the things you say. And for your own personal development it is best if you learn to say it.

Don't Drop the Conversational Ball

When questions are opened up to you, take your cue and express yourself with an adequate answer. Monosyllabic replies of "yes" and "no" and "maybe" discourage conversation. Keep in mind that it takes more than the other person to keep a good conversation going. You must do your part.

Edith, for example, was a college girl — pretty and very talented. But she was so painfully shy that she could not carry on an acceptable conversation unless it was with someone she knew extremely well. Because she was nice looking and was blessed with unusual ability, many of the college boys were attracted to her. However, she was seldom dated more than once or twice by the same boy — and after a while the word got around that she was a "bore." The truth of the matter was that Edith was intelligent and very interesting — but she was too timid to express herself. Others who wanted to cultivate her friendship found it too difficult to break through the wall of silence that surrounded her. Thus, she was cut off from what she needed the most — friends. And all because she would not talk.

Participating in friendly discussions, expressing your opinions, exchanging your ideas and sharing your experiences all help you become a fluent conversationalist. This in turn will add to your confidence.

Don't Expect a Special Invitation to Join in a Conversation

If you are a shy person, others may not direct their conversation to you. But that does not mean that they would not be happy to talk with you. In fact, they may be just as shy as you are, waiting for you to start the discussion. As a mature adult it is your responsibility to "break the ice" and speak a friendly word. Actually, in most informal groups *no one* is invited to start talking. But neither are two people, or a group, expected to sit without employing their social skills and enjoying a pleasant time together. So if you are in a strange group or seated near someone you do not know very well, do not hesitate to open the conversation with a few words. People not only *like* to talk, they *need* to talk; and by initiating a conversation you are helping others as well as yourself.

It is all well to be a good listener, but there are times when you should speak up and actively participate in a conversation. Don't just *think* what you would like to say — *say it!* When you do, life will not only become more interesting for you, but you will find yourself accepted *in* the group rather than on the periphery. This will add greatly to your self-confidence.

Be Cheerful and Optimistic

The Scriptures say, "A merry heart doeth good like a medicine: but a broken spirit drieth the bones" (Proverbs 17:22). A cheerful person adds much to any group. An optimistic outlook always wears well. As you may have noticed, people are attracted to those who see the bright side of things. On the contrary, people tend to avoid those who continually criticize or bear the burden of the whole world upon their shoulders. You have heard people say, "I don't like to be around him. He's always complaining about something." On the other hand, people may say, "Did you ever see such a cheerful, happy person? Just being around him is a tonic." A man once confided to a friend that he had served as a board member for a certain organization during the past twelve months, and he knew one man on the board who had never made one constructive remark! Attending the same meetings, he pointed out, there were two people who during the year's time had never failed to speak an *encouraging* word.

The Christian need not try to muster up an artificial optimism. With Christ as one's Saviour, an optimistic outlook is built in. The child of God has everything to be cheerful about. Christ is his Saviour, God is on the throne, and he is on the victory side. As a Christian, one should be happy in the Lord, and his conversation should echo his inner peace and joy.

Talk About the Lord

Ask the Holy Spirit to guide you into a discussion of Christ and what He means to you. There is no better subject. When talking with others, tell something of your own experience with the Lord. This is first-hand information and it cannot be refuted. Because it is your *personal experience,* it will be of interest to those with whom you speak.

Very often the mention of a Christian college or a special evangelical crusade will elicit a worthwhile discussion. Dick, for example, was a quiet person who found it difficult to initiate a conversation. One day, however, seated next to a stranger on an airliner, he felt that he should speak to this person about Christ. But it was painful to get started. Quietly he prayed, asking God to wedge open the conversation. Holding a newspaper in his hand, Dick came across a photo of a well-known evangelist. *This is it,* he thought. *I'll mention the picture and article to this man.* He did, and much to his surprise found that his seatmate was somewhat interested in the same article. One remark led to another, and in a few minutes Dick was witnessing to this man about the Lord. Before leaving the plane, Dick gave his new "friend" a copy of a tract that he always carried with him.

For some time afterward Dick thought about the man and prayed for him. How glad he was that he had obeyed God and had forced himself to open the conversation and to talk about the Lord!

4 | Confidence Through Christ

Two psychologists were talking one day about the theories of change.

"Do you know what our biggest problem is?" asked one.

"What's on your mind?"

"Just this: as psychologists we can give examinations, study people, then come up with scientific findings. But here's the rub — we can't *change* people."

And this psychologist was right. We *can* and *do* help people alter their attitudes — at least to some degree. But basic changes of character and personality are jobs much too big for human beings. These are tasks for God. Attitudes of confidence can be improved to some extent by various self-helps. But thoroughgoing changes come only as you commit your problem to the Lord — the One who made and fashioned you.

Since man's loss of royal privileges in Eden, the idea of "self-confidence" has the doubtful suggestion of trusting in oneself rather than the omnipotent wisdom of God. But when we recognize our own utter weakness and place our faith and confidence completely in God, we find that the glories of life are virtually without limit. Christians have every reason to be confident because their confidence is in the living God — the Creator of the universe.

Peace of Mind

In today's troubled world we hear much about *"peace of mind."* Tranquilizers and drugs are generally considered acceptable crutches for the relief of personal tension and restlessness. Yet, permanent peace of mind must come from within. Only as our sins are forgiven and Christ dwells in our hearts can we know true peace of mind — the kind that endures and sets our spirits free.

Research has never contradicted the fact that people are born with sinful natures. Rather, all evidence points insistently to the fact that the human race has a bent toward sinning. It is the most natural thing in the world for people to do wrong. Why? Because it is their nature. Man has a built-in tendency to sin. This does not mean that man does not possess great potential or have many good points. And it does not mean that we are continuously committing serious crimes. But it *does* mean that not one of us is able to stand in the presence of a holy God.

So it is that God, because of His great love for us, made a provision whereby each one of us can get *right* with God and have our sins forgiven. He gave His Son, the Lord Jesus Christ, to die on the cross for us. When we trust in Him, He gives us a new nature and a new life. This new nature is the result of being "born again." The first birth is physical, the second, spiritual. We are born first of our parents; then we are born again into the family of God when we trust in Christ as our personal Saviour. This spiritual rebirth is what changes people's sinful natures.

We read in Romans 3:23: "For all have sinned, and come short of the glory of God." Romans 6:23 says, "For the wages of sin is death, but the gift of God is eternal life through Jesus Christ, our Lord."

We read in Ephesians 2:8,9, that we cannot save ourselves: "For by grace are ye saved through faith; and that not of yourselves: it is the gift of God: Not of works, lest any man should boast."

But God has graciously made a wonderful provision: "For God so loved the world, that he gave his only begotten Son, that whosoever believeth in him should not perish, but have everlasting life" (John 3:16).

Yet, even with God's marvelous provision, it is still possible for us to go our own way without committing our lives to Him. Our part is simply to surrender, then ask Him to save us. "For whosoever shall call upon the name of the Lord shall be saved" (Romans 10:13).

Through the centuries countless multitudes have called upon Christ and He has saved them. It is the most scientifically proven fact in history!

But what does getting right with God have to do with confidence? A great deal. Yes, more than anything else. First, we have FORGIVENESS—a *forgiven past,* a *clean present,* and an *optimistic future!* No one can feel confident when he is burdened 'neath a load of sin. But when he knows that his sins are forgiven, it gives him confidence in his relationship with God and man. God says, "For as the heaven is high above the earth, so great is his mercy toward them that fear him. As far as the east is from the west, so far hath he removed our transgressions from us" (Psalm 103:11,12).

When we accept Christ as our personal Saviour, the Holy Spirit comes into our hearts to dwell. We have a new nature. Does this mean that we become perfect? No, but we do have a perfect standing in Christ.

Indeed, personal confidence thrives on *peace of mind*. And since genuine tranquility stems from a knowledge of sins forgiven, no one has or ever will be able to find a substitute for the peace that emanates from God.

"Come now, and let us reason together, saith the Lord: though your sins be as scarlet, they shall be as white as snow; though they be red like crimson, they shall be as wool" (Isaiah 1:18).

Strangely, it is not only the non-Christian but often the Christian who seemingly will not let God forgive him. This may sometimes be traced to the image of a parent or some other person who could not forgive. Jack, for example, remembered unconsciously the life-long grudge his father held against certain family members. Jack had been saved for several years, but God remained a larger projection of his own father — a limited revelation of God indeed, but quite natural to one who did not yet understand God's perfections. Thus, Jack could not seem to believe that God had really forgiven *him*.

The whole course of Jack's life was turned to a fruitful confidence in God when he began to study and finally believe God's Word. It happened as God spoke to him about the word "all." The passage was familiar, but it suddenly became personal. The torment of doubt left as he read with joy, "If we confess our sins, he is faithful and just to forgive us our sins, and to cleanse us from *all* unrighteousness" (I John 1:9).

Our Position in Christ

Salvation brings something else which gives us unusual confidence — *position* in Him. When we trust in Christ, God becomes our Father and we become His sons. "But as many as received him, to them gave he power to become the sons of God, even to them that believe on his name" (John 1:12). God also says that we are "heirs of God" and "joint-heirs with Christ" (Romans 8:17). In addition, we are a royal priesthood. Confidence? Yes. There is no greater confidence!

How wonderful to realize that as Christians we find ourselves *in* Christ. We also discover that we are *in* the Father's hand: "I give unto them eternal life; and they shall never perish, neither shall any man pluck them out of my hand. My Father, which gave them me, is greater than all; and no man is able to pluck them out of my Father's hand" (John 10:28,29).

With such assurance, no one need cower under pressure brought on by lack of confidence. Indeed, as children of the Heavenly King, we have every reason to be confident.

Pseudo religious cults and many godless practitioners of psychiatry and psychological counseling have asserted a monopoly on positive thinking! In actual fact, all such teachings outside of God's mandate to His redeemed ones are fleeting and futile. True, these principles bring some temporary benefit in a swiftly-deteriorating material existence. How much more, then, on an infinite plane do they work marvelously in God's eternal plan, being linked with His divine Son who was crucified and risen.

Why make counterfeit self assurance when a real foundation for confidence is available? There is not much enduring profit in whistling by grave yards, or playing Pollyanna in a world of death and ruin. Infinitely better than trying to assert fallen mind over fallen matter is the blood-washed Christian's title deed to permanent confidence over every circumstance and adversity.

Take Hebrews 11:1 (Amplified New Testament), for example: "Now faith is the assurance (the confirmation, the title-deed) of the things [we] hope for, being the proof of things [we] do not see *and* the conviction of their reality — faith perceiving as real fact what is not revealed to the senses."

What a source of rich confidence! How could a life refuse the wholesome fact of this radiant announcement? It ought to inspire limitless confidence. It is better than the sum of every human treasure, and infinitely more practical.

God's Word frequently repeats these assurances in judicial, biological, and picture language so that there is no reason for the Christian to live without confidence. The cumulative argument is that the child of God has the resources of the Heavenly Father *now*, as well as for eternity.

When Rudyard Kipling was a lad, he went on a sea voyage with his father, Lockwood Kipling. Soon after the vessel got under way, Mr. Kipling went below, leaving Rudyard on deck. Presently there was a great commotion overhead, and one of the officers ran down and banged on Mr. Kipling's door.

"Mr. Kipling," he cried, "your boy has crawled out on the yardarm, and if he let's go, he'll drown!"

"Yes," said Mr. Kipling confidently, "but I know my son. He won't let go."

So it is with our position in Christ. Danger and difficulty may surround us, but we know our Lord!

Eternal Life

With the assurance of eternal life comes immeasurable confidence. Here is a boon that is utterly unknown to any heathen religion or human philosophy. Gnawed with gloomy misgivings, men have dreamed of immortality. Yet, God alone is the source of it — the implementation. Christ is risen from the dead, and because He lives, we as His redeemed ones have eternal life through Him.

Confidence is bright for those who have already entered this eternal family, and who know that with the soon coming of their Lord and Saviour, Jesus Christ, they will be transformed into His risen likeness.

As a Christian you can say, "For I am persuaded, that neither death, nor life, nor angels, nor principalities, nor powers, nor things present, nor things to come, nor height, nor depth, nor any other creature, shall be able to separate us from the love of God, which is in Christ Jesus our Lord" (Romans 8:38,39).

There is a beautiful story told of McLeod Campbell, the Scotch preacher. One day a friend came to him in spiritual perplexity. "Tell me, how do you know that you always have hold of God?" For a moment the minister was silent, and then, with a great wistfulness in his eyes, he said: "How do I know that I always have hold of God? I don't always know; but I do know He always has hold of me!"

Divine Guidance

Unless they are in the fold of God, human beings are like straying sheep. They have lost their bearing. But the Good Shepherd gives divine guidance and unerring direction toward the future — confidence regardless of the circumstances. God promises, "I will instruct thee and teach thee in the way which thou shalt go: I will guide thee with mine eye" (Psalm 32:8).

Jerry often thought of the time he would choose a life partner. Although he was but a young man, he had perfect confidence that God would direct his path, and he was never disappointed. He was spared many pitfalls as he kept God's Word in his heart. At a summer camp he met Gwen, a lovely Christian girl who had also committed the leadership of her life to the Lord. Several years later they were married and established a Christian home. So it is with all young people who trust God for guidance in their plans for marriage. They can take the wedding vows in utmost confidence, being assured that God has given what is best for them.

Christian young couples everywhere can enter marriage with the confident knowledge that God, who brought them together, can guide them into paths of blessing if they will only turn to Him in complete dependence.

What a source of confidence it is to realize that God is interested in every area of a Christian's life. Whether it be in the choice of a school, a decision about one's work, or a problem in training the children, Christ walks beside us to give unerring guidance and to lead us in the paths that are best.

A story is told of two men who were attempting to scale a great mountain. The climber had come to a perilous gap in the ice where the only way to get across was to place his

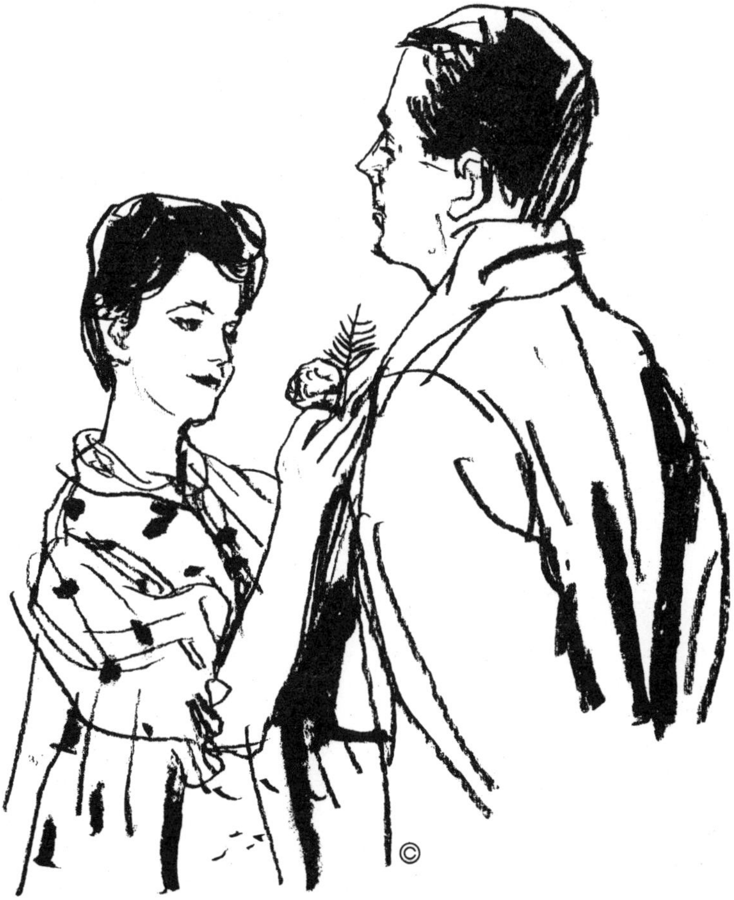

foot in the outstretched hand of the guide. Told to do this by the guide, the climber hesitated a moment as he looked into the gloomy depths below. Seeing the hesitation, the guide said, "Have no fear, sir; that hand never yet lost a man." With this assurance the traveler trusted the guide and crossed safely over. So it is with us. The soul that truly commits itself into the hands of Jesus Christ is committed to the strong, sure keeping of hands that have never yet lost a man. And they never will! He is our *sure Guide*.

God's Provision
A missionary was teaching a class of Navajo boys to say the Twenty-third Psalm. When Bahi's turn came, he started out confidently, "The Lord is my Shepherd, I've got all I want." This was well stated. It showed complete confidence in God's provision as well as completeness of desire!

Indeed, as children of God we can live in the daily confidence that God is our Father and will meet our needs. We can rest confidently in *God's provision*. "And my God will liberally supply (fill to the full) your every need according to His riches in glory in Christ Jesus" (Philippians 4:19. *Amplified New Testament*).

Christian confidence reposes in the resources of both heaven and earth. They are dispensed by our guardian, the Holy Spirit, not according to our desire (which might easily lead us astray); but according to our *needs*. God does not promise to give us all that we want, or all that we *think* we need — but He does say that He will supply all our needs. And they will not be according to our own material riches, but according to His divine wealth and eternal storehouse.

And that is not all. Because God knows our every need (even better than we do ourselves) He provides us with many things that have not even entered the crevices of our minds. For example, in Luke 21:15, God promises, "I will give you a mouth and wisdom, which all your adversaries shall not be able to gainsay or resist."

We can join with the apostle Paul in saying, "I can do all things through Christ which strengtheneth me" (Philippians 4:13). How wonderful it is that God provides us with the strength to do the things that He calls us to do.

God gave His Son, who in turn paid for all our sins upon the cross of Calvary. God is a loving and a gracious

Father who provides for His own. He has never changed since He fed the multitudes of Israel in the wilderness, giving them enough manna for each day and supplying water from the rock.

In a desperate longing for security, and without confidence in God, there are obviously not enough kinds of insurance to hedge mankind from common troubles, let alone eternal sorrow. A recent writer proved that a well-to-do American cannot even afford the sum of insurance premiums now required by the hazards thought necessary for coverage — fire, life, theft, collision, liability, tornado, earthquake, unemployment, travel, hospital, surgery, and scores of others. But God sees every sparrow that falls and He numbers the hairs of our heads. He loves His children and He cares for His own. Listen to His voice:

> Therefore I tell you, stop being perpetually uneasy (anxious and worried) about your life, what you shall eat *or what you shall drink,* and about your body, what you shall put on. Is not life greater [in quality] than food, and the body [far above and more excellent] than clothing?
>
> Look at the birds of the air; they neither sow nor reap nor gather into barns, and yet your heavenly Father keeps feeding them. Are you not worth more than they?
>
> And which of you by worrying and being anxious can add one unit of measure [cubit] to his stature *or* to the span of his life?
>
> And why should you be anxious about clothes? Consider the lilies of the field *and* learn thoroughly how they grow; they neither toil nor spin;
>
> Yet I tell you, even Solomon in all his magnificence (excellence, dignity and grace) was not arrayed like one of these.
>
> But if God so clothes the grass of the field, which today is alive and green *and* tomorrow is tossed into the furnace, will He not much more surely clothe you, O you men with little faith?
>
> Therefore do not worry *and* be anxious, saying, What are we going to have to eat? or, What are we going to have to drink? or, What are we going to have to wear?
>
> For the Gentiles (heathen) wish for *and* crave *and* diligently seek after all these things; and your heavenly Father well knows that you need them all.
>
> But seek for (aim at and strive after) first of all His kingdom, and His righteousness (His way of doing and being right), and then all these things taken together will be given you besides.
>
> So do not worry *or* be anxious about tomorrow, for tomorrow will have worries *and* anxieties of its own. Sufficient for each day is its own trouble. (Matthew 6:25-34. *Amplified New Testament*).

Indeed, we have a great God, and when our confidence is in Him, we have nothing to fear. Each day as we read God's Word and remain close to His side, our hearts and minds are flooded with the realization that we have peace of mind, a special position in Christ, eternal life, divine guidance, and God's provision. Through Christ we can walk *assuredly*.

5 | Understanding Your Feelings

Self-confidence hangs largely on how we feel about ourselves. Naturally, if we want to increase our self-confidence, we must take a close look at our feelings. We cannot expect to move forward until we *understand* our attitudes. This approach is in keeping with the psychological principles that (1) all behavior is caused, and (2) causes are always multiple.

In other words, you don't just *happen* to feel as you do. There are actually many years of experiences that have slowly but surely shaped your attitudes. They may have come so early and so subtly that you were not aware of them. But these experiences were definite in creating your present feelings, and now it may seem that you are helpless to overcome or change them.

As you look for the causes of your attitudes, scan the horizon for all the possible causes of your diffidence. Look for several reasons, not just one. Undoubtedly there have been a number of dynamics that have been at work to produce your present reactions. So make sure you identify the multiple causations.

To uncover the causes of shyness, it is sometimes helpful to enlist the cooperation of a close friend. Is there someone who is confidential and with whom you can talk freely? If so, don't overlook such a person. In many cases a husband

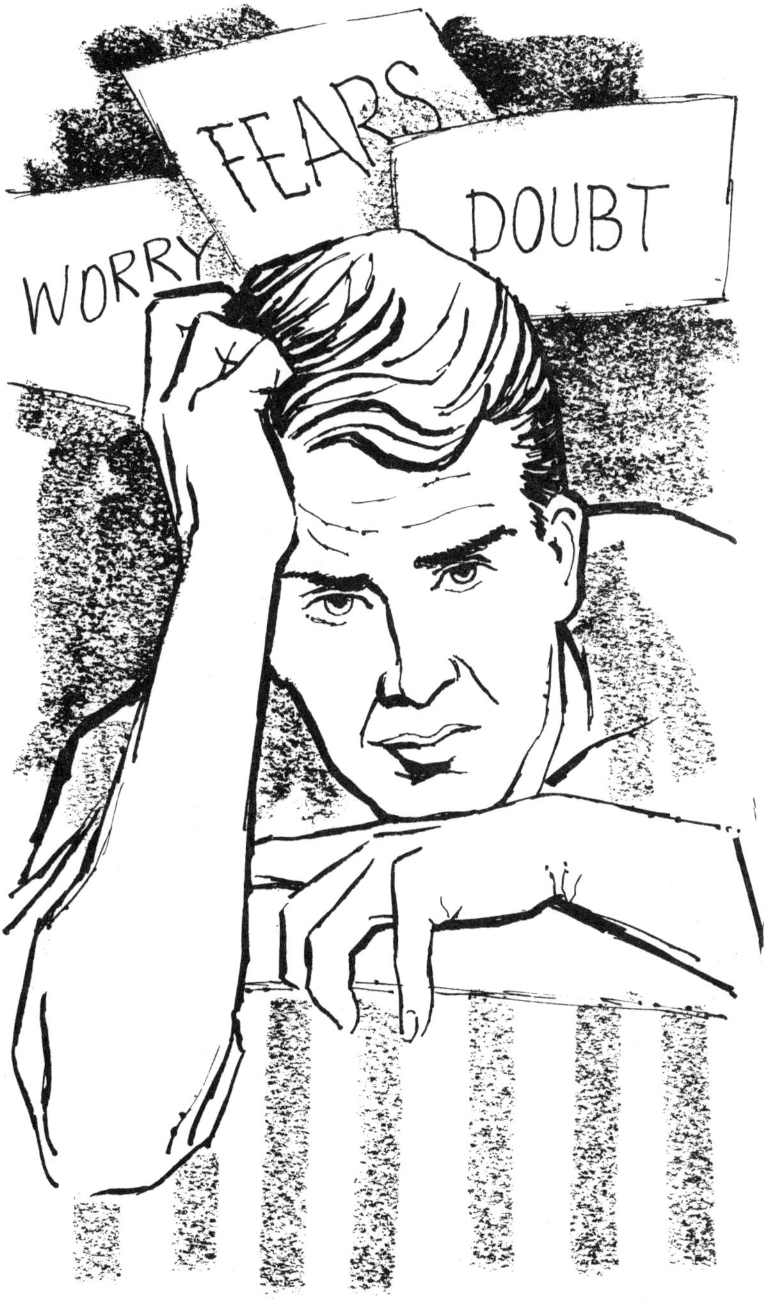
FEARS
DOUBT
WORRY

or a wife is the best one with whom to discuss your problem. In other instances, it may be an understanding relative or some friend with whom you feel especially comfortable.

By discussing your situation thoroughly, you may discover certain experiences in your childhood or teen years which contributed to your present attitudes and feelings. As you bring them out in the open and talk about them, you may recall many other instances that also affected you. One insight usually leads to another. But deep insights seldom emerge in the first or second discussion. It may require a number of such times before the hidden causes are brought to light.

As you discover the reasons why you lack confidence, and as you ventilate your feelings, they will probably begin to disappear. A rationalized and thought-through problem usually loses its hold on a person. As you gain self-understanding, you will also develop more self-confidence.

Take Harriet, for example. Her extreme shyness restricted her in all that she did. Eventually she met a fine Christian girl with whom she later shared an apartment. Harriet's roommate sensed how painfully shy Harriet was. As the months passed they had many long talks. For the first time in her life Harriet began to understand the true basis for her feelings of timidity. Gradually she discovered the experiences which had caused her to turn inward to herself. As she brought these hidden facts out into the open and discussed them, she realized how ungrounded these attitudes were. As she continued this process her outlook changed, and she gained more self-confidence.

Like Harriet, you, too, can learn the true causes of your feelings. As you do, you will begin to feel differently and see things in a clearer perspective. Then you will have the freedom to act differently. Your fears and feelings of insecurity will gradually give way to attitudes of confidence.

6 | Seeking Professional Help

In some instances a person's confidence is destroyed so completely, or is so utterly lacking, that he should seek professional help.

A person may rationalize, "If I can't lick this problem myself, no one else can do it for me." But such reasoning is faulty. If a person had a sprained ankle or an injured back, he would not hesitate to seek medical assistance. Should one be any less practical when dealing with personality problems? Indeed, when we need help we should, by all means, get it.

Intelligent people know that they can receive much benefit from one who is professionally trained in matters of personality structure. A physician, psychologist, psychiatrist, or a well-trained minister can do much to help a person overcome maladjustments.

Extreme shyness is sometimes centered in hidden health problems. On the other hand, it may stem from mental or emotional instability. Other times lack of confidence is an indication of a deeper, spiritual need. More often than not, however, it is the result of a combination of forces. If the basis for lack of confidence is psychological in origin, the therapist will encourage you to discuss your situation fully and bring to light the experiences that have caused you to feel as you do.

But this takes time. A number of sessions may be required to unearth the causes, and to reconstruct new patterns of thinking and acting.

Consider Betty, who was the essence of timidity. She had worried for years about her problem, but no hope was in sight. Finally, after reading an article about another woman who had received help from a Christian psychologist, she decided to seek help for herself. She went, had a number of appointments, and saw that she could be helped. In fact, she enjoyed her visits. In time she rid herself of the attitudes which were preventing her from becoming the first-rate person that she was capable of being.

Is professional help expensive? Not in comparison to the value. And the minimum investment for a few months is nothing compared to the life-time benefits one receives. Like Betty, if you need professional help, you cannot afford *not* to have it.

If you have a serious problem involving lack of confidence that has stubbornly persisted through the years and crippled your efficiency, it is only reasonable to seek professional counsel. In all probability, you will be amazed at the changes that take place in your attitudes and personality when your problem is accurately diagnosed and treated.

Many have benefited from professional help. You can too!

7 | In Retrospect

God wants us to be confident. The life that Christ gives the believer is intended to be vibrant and full — not timid and fearful. Jesus said, "I came that they may have and enjoy life, and have it in abundance — to the full, till it overflows (John 10:10 *Amplified New Testament*).

Lack of confidence, or perhaps better termed, "personality defeat," is devastating not only because it crushes a person, but because this serious maladjustment affects one's children as well. When a child is raised by a parent who feels inadequate, the son or daughter usually suffers, too.

The breaking of this vicious circle can begin with *you*. Realize that competence and confidence go hand-in-hand. As you deliberately develop your abilities, you can be secure in the knowledge that, in comparison to others, you rate high as a capable person.

When you look right, you usually feel right. Knowing that your appearance is attractive and appropriate gives you confidence that frees you from yourself and allows you to tackle the interesting jobs at hand. You will not be preoccupied with worries about how you look when you know that you are well groomed and make an acceptable appearance.

Feeling at ease comes largely through the development of socially-accepted manners. Crudeness, or a lack of knowledge of proper etiquette only calls attention to yourself, causing you to be self-conscious or to use compensational behavior. But as you develop natural, cordial manners, you will gain poise which is so necessary for self-assurance. But if and when you *do* make an error, remember that how you take it will spell the difference between poise and lack of self-confidence.

Analyze and understand your own feelings. Realize that other people may not even know that you are especially shy. In fact, they may be timid themselves.

Probably nothing reveals our true selves more than does our speech. All our background, attitudes, intelligence, and spirituality are bound up in our conversational skills. In addition, scarcely anything helps a person put his best foot forward as effectively as the ability to carry on an interesting conversation. This fosters confidence.

Yet, with all these other techniques, the most thoroughgoing change that can come to you is that which is wrought by the Holy Spirit. Man is born to believe and follow God. As he does, he becomes heir to an endless wealth of benefits. As you walk daily with the Saviour, you will gain an inner strength and confidence in the Lord that will reveal itself in all you do.

In some instances, lack of self-confidence is actually mistaken for a more serious condition — emotional or mental illness. At times it is mistaken for a physical disorder. If such is true, the solution comes in seeking professional diagnosis, followed by prescribed medication or appropriate counseling therapy.

Confidence is not a lacquer applied to the outside of your personality. It's much more than that. It is a result product that has its roots down deep. Confidence is the outworking of an internal condition — the natural fruit of a mature personality.

And it can be yours!